WHEN PLANET EARTH WAS NEW

WHEN PLANET EARTH WAS NEW

WRITTEN BY
JAMES GLADSTONE

ILLUSTRATED BY
KATHERINE DIEMERT

OWLKIDS BOOKS

THIS WAS EARTH ...

LONG BEFORE PLANTS,
ANIMALS, OR PEOPLE ...

BILLIONS OF YEARS AGO ...

WHEN PLANET EARTH
WAS NEW.

YOU COULD NOT WALK
ON THE SEARING-HOT
MOLTEN ROCK THAT
FLOWED THERE ...

OR BREATHE THE DEADLY
POISON GAS THAT
SWIRLED THERE.

NOTHING COULD.

THERE WAS NO LIFE
ON EARTH WHEN PLANET
EARTH WAS NEW.

MILLIONS OF YEARS PASSED ...

AND SLOWLY — SO SLOWLY — EARTH STARTED TO COOL.

THE HOT LIQUID ROCK BECAME SOLID.

A SKY FULL OF WATER VAPOR
POURED DOWN AS RAIN.

FOR MILLIONS AND MILLIONS
AND MILLIONS OF YEARS,
IT RAINED.

THE RAIN FORMED
HUGE OCEANS.

THE OCEANS ARE WHERE
LIFE FIRST GREW.

TINY LIFE-FORMS GREW
INTO MATS OF SLIMY GREEN.
THEY FORMED MOUNDS OF
STRANGE ROCK.

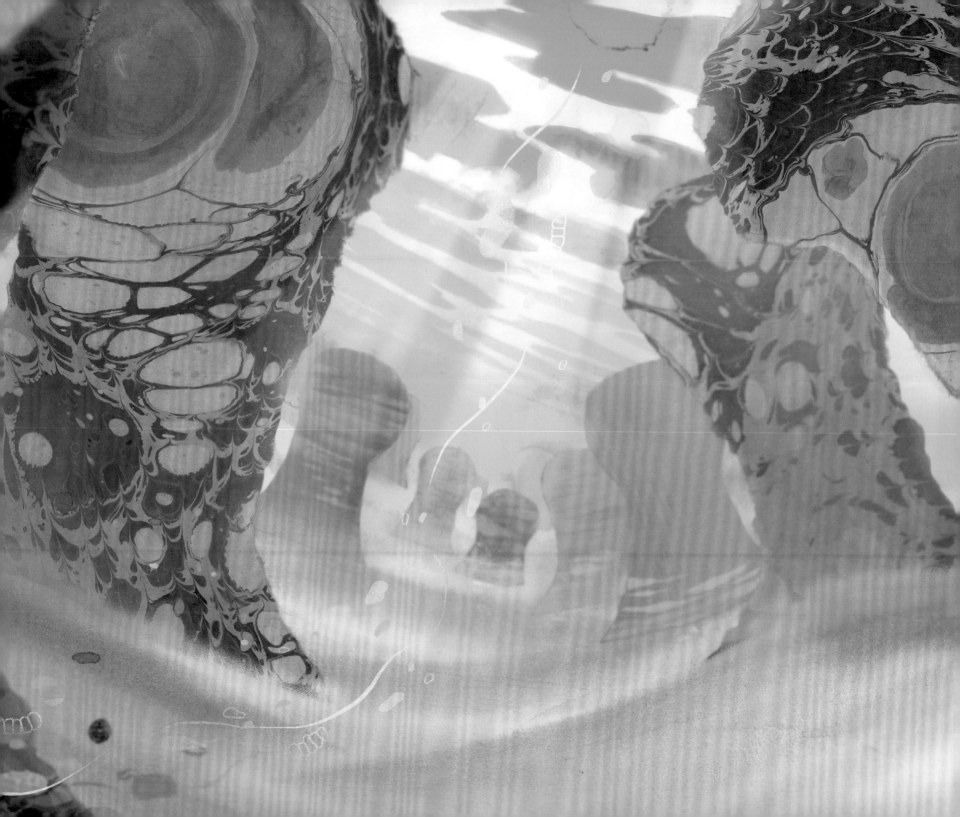

FOR MILLIONS AND MILLIONS
AND MILLIONS OF YEARS,
THESE SMALL FORMS OF LIFE
DID SOMETHING QUITE BIG.

THEY HELPED MAKE THE
OXYGEN IN THE AIR—
THE OXYGEN THAT YOU
BREATHE, AND THAT ALL
ANIMALS NEED TO LIVE.

LIFE EVOLVED IN THE OCEANS.

LIFE EVOLVED ON LAND.

BUT EARTH'S GREAT GLOBE
OF LIFE DID NOT EVOLVE
ALL AT ONCE.

CAN YOU GUESS?

IT TOOK MILLIONS AND
MILLIONS AND MILLIONS
OF YEARS FOR ANCIENT
LIFE TO EVOLVE.

THROUGH ALL THIS
TIME, ANCIENT SPECIES
LIVED AND THRIVED.

THROUGH ALL
THIS TIME, ANCIENT
SPECIES WENT EXTINCT.
THEIR KIND DIED.

IT TOOK MILLIONS AND
MILLIONS AND MILLIONS
OF YEARS MORE ...

...TO EVOLVE THE LIFE WE SEE ON EARTH TODAY.

LIFE THAT INCLUDES PEOPLE LIKE YOU AND ME.

PEOPLE NOW LIVE ALL OVER THE WORLD.

IT MAY SEEM AS IF WE HAVE BEEN HERE FOREVER.

BUT HUMAN LIFE IS A SPECK IN TIME IN THE HISTORY OF OLD EARTH.

THIS IS EARTH TODAY, NOW
BILLIONS OF YEARS OLDER.

IT IS GREENER AND BLUER,
MORE COMFORTABLE AND
MUCH COOLER ...

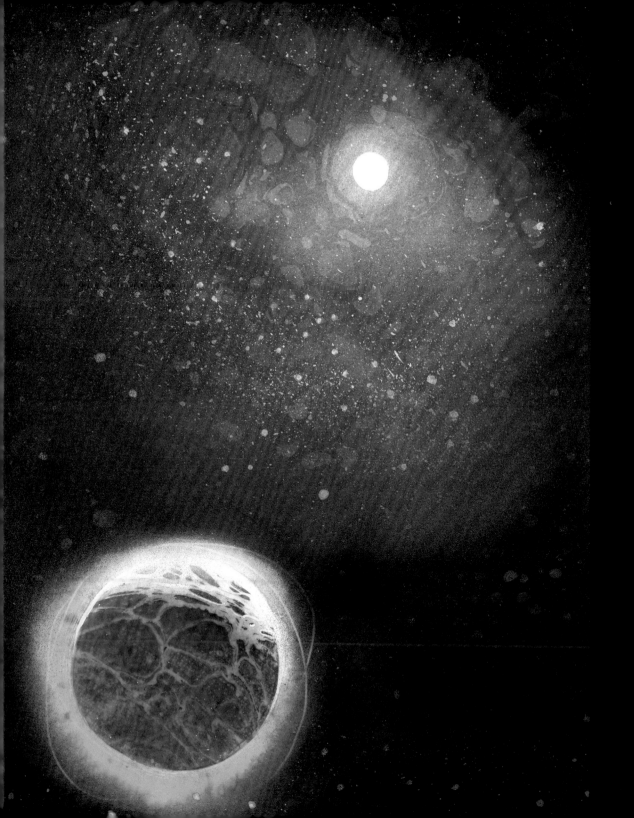

... THAN WHEN PLANET
EARTH WAS NEW.

LOOK AGAIN

Look back through the book. Page by page, here are some of the things you can see as Earth changes and becomes the place it is today.

You are looking at Earth billions of years ago, when it was a very young planet. Rivers of lava glow on its surface. Comets and asteroids fly through the solar system. Some even hit Earth. You can see the Sun in the distance.

Volcanoes erupt. Bubbling lava explodes into the air, and dark clouds fill the sky. Earth is burning hot and covered in molten rock. Many comets crash into Earth. The gases in the atmosphere make the sky look orange.

This is Earth's surface. Mountains poke out from the mist. During the day, their peaks are lit by the rays of the Sun. There are fewer active volcanoes now, and less lava flows from them. The Moon hangs in the night sky over the still-lifeless planet.

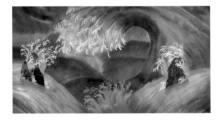

As Earth cools, water vapor in the atmosphere condenses into liquid. Clouds fill the sky and rain pours down. So much rain falls that it collects on Earth's surface and forms the oceans. Towering waves crash and roll.

You are looking under water. The tiny, single-celled forms of life you see have many different shapes. The mounds of rock on the ocean floor are called stromatolites. They are formed by cyanobacteria in the water. Look up toward the ocean's surface. There you can see mats of cyanobacteria.

The setting Sun reflects off the water. Fields of stromatolites poke above the water's surface. Mats of cyanobacteria float on the water near the shore.

The oceans are bursting with life. Corals, plants, fish, and many other creatures large and small grow and thrive in Earth's waters.

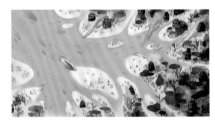

Life, which first grew in the oceans, begins to move onto land. Plants and invertebrate animals evolve on land first. Later, larger animals evolve on land, feeding on the rich plant life.

Life on Earth continues to evolve in amazing ways. Fish, water creatures, trees and other plant life, large insects, and reptiles all flourish. There are even early dinosaurs. Do you see the creatures that slither and crawl on the tree trunk?

Small and large plant- and meat-eaters roam Earth—it is the age of the dinosaurs. Some of these creatures take to the air and soar through Earth's skies.

The dinosaurs have died off. Their bones are all that's left behind. But there is still life on Earth. Do you see the creature that is wandering the sand dunes?

Life on Earth is thriving. Look in and around the tree. There are many kinds of mammals. Do you see the birds? They evolved from small dinosaurs.

Earth abounds with creatures. Animals are found in the sea, in the sky, and on land. Do you recognize the creatures on parade? One of them should be very familiar— it's a human being. People now live on Earth.

Humans raise buildings, create cities, and develop modes of transportation, such as boats and cars. These changes mean parts of the planet are no longer wild, as they once were.

You're looking down on Earth. Do you see the bright blue of the oceans and the vibrant green of the land? The Sun is setting on the horizon.

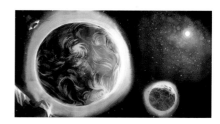

This is Earth today, as seen from outer space. It is no longer hot and lifeless. Oceans and landmasses cover the planet. You can see our Moon and Sun too. It has taken millions and millions and millions of years for Earth to become the planet it is today. And it isn't finished. Plants and animals are still evolving. Planet Earth is still changing.

GLOSSARY

ancient: From a time in the distant past.

asteroid: A rock that goes around the Sun. Larger asteroids can be as big as a huge city. Smaller asteroids can be the size of an elephant.

atmosphere: All of the air that surrounds Earth.

cell: A very small unit of life. All living things are made up of cells. Some living things are made of one cell, while others, such as people, are made of trillions of cells.

comet: A big ball of frozen gas, rock, and dust that goes around the Sun.

condense: To change from a gas to a liquid by cooling.

coral: Tiny, colorful creatures that attach themselves to rocks on the sea floor.

cyanobacteria: An early form of microscopic life in the oceans.

evolve: To change or develop over time.

extinct: Used to refer to a species of animal or plant that has died out and no longer exists.

gas: A substance that is not a solid or a liquid. Oxygen, for example, is a gas that makes up part of the air we breathe.

invertebrate: An animal that does not have a backbone.

lava: Melted rock that comes from a volcano.

mammal: An animal that is a warm-blooded vertebrate with hair. A human being is a mammal.

microscopic: Something that is too small to be seen with the naked eye. Scientists use microscopes to see microscopic objects.

molten: Used to refer to materials that are turned into liquid by heating.

oxygen: A gas without color or smell that makes up part of the air we breathe.

solar system: Our Sun and all the planets, moons, comets, and asteroids that move around it.

species: A group of similar animals or plants that can make offspring together.

stromatolite: A layered mound of rock that forms in shallow waters.

vertebrate: An animal that has a backbone.

volcano: An opening in Earth's surface from which lava, rock, and gases erupt.

water vapor: The gas form of water. Ice is a solid form of water. Rain is a liquid form of water.

AUTHOR'S NOTE

In the deep, deep past, Earth was a hot, lifeless, alien world. That was the idea that first sparked my interest in writing this book.

The incredible changes that have occurred over more than 4.5 billion years have taken Earth from its boiling beginnings to the living planet we know today. My goal was to tell that story of change. I wanted to capture, in a picture book, the grand spectacle of Earth's sweep forward through vast stretches of time. Much to my delight, Katherine Diemert's imaginative and powerful illustrations have brought that vision to life more beautifully than I could have hoped for.

In the pages of *When Planet Earth Was New*, we hope to excite your interest in Earth's story, instill wonder at the variety of life that has evolved over eons, and—more than anything—share the thrill of imagining planet Earth when it was new!

Acknowledgement

Many thanks to Michael Benton, Professor of Vertebrate Palaeontology and Head of School of Biological Sciences, University of Bristol, UK, for reviewing the illustrations—and for reminding us that evolution is a bush, not a line.

SOURCES

Books

Benton, Michael J. *The History of Life: A Very Short Introduction.* Oxford: Oxford University Press, 2008.

Gribbin, John. *Planet Earth: A Beginner's Guide.* London: Oneworld Publications, 2012.

Redfern, Martin. *The Earth: A Very Short Introduction*. Oxford: Oxford University Press, 2003.

Woolfson, Michael M. *Time, Space, Stars & Man: The Story of the Big Bang*. 2nd ed. London: Imperial College Press, 2013.

Websites

BBC. "Find Out How the Earth Works."
http://www.bbc.co.uk/science/earth

BBC. "The Late Heavy Bombardment Ends."
http://www.bbc.co.uk/science/earth/earth_timeline/late_heavy_bombardment

NASA Space Place. "Explore Earth and Space."
http://spaceplace.nasa.gov/

National Geographic. "Mass Extinctions: What Causes Animal Die-Offs?"
http://science.nationalgeographic.com/science/prehistoric-world/mass-extinction/

National Geographic. "Prehistoric Time Line."
http://science.nationalgeographic.com/science/prehistoric-world/prehistoric-time-line/

PBS. "Evolution: Deep Time."
http://www.pbs.org/wgbh/evolution/change/deeptime/

Smithsonian National Museum of Natural History. "The Ocean Throughout Geologic Time: An Image Gallery."
ocean.si.edu/slideshow/ocean-throughout-geologic-time-image-gallery

FOR DAD, WHO LOVES TO MAKE AND READ BOOKS — J.G.

FOR MUM AND DAD, WHO GAVE ME THE WORLD — K.D.

Owlkids Books acknowledges the financial support of the Canada Council for the Arts, the Ontario Arts Council, the Government of Canada through the Canada Book Fund (CBF) and the Government of Ontario through the Ontario Media Development Corporation's Book Initiative for our publishing activities.

Published in Canada by
Owlkids Books Inc.
10 Lower Spadina Avenue
Toronto, ON M5V 2Z2

Published in the United States by
Owlkids Books Inc.
1700 Fourth Street
Berkeley, CA 94710

ONTARIO ARTS COUNCIL
CONSEIL DES ARTS DE L'ONTARIO
an Ontario government agency
un organisme du gouvernement de l'Ontario

Canada Council   Conseil des Arts
for the Arts   du Canada

Canada

Library and Archives Canada Cataloguing in Publication

Gladstone, James, 1969-, author
    When planet Earth was new / written by James Gladstone ; illustrated by Katherine Diemert.

ISBN 978-1-77147-203-6 (hardcover)

    1. Earth (Planet)--Juvenile literature. 2. Earth (Planet)--History--Juvenile literature. 3. Earth (Planet)--Origin--Juvenile literature. 4. Historical geology--Juvenile literature. 5. Life--Origin--Juvenile literature. 6. Natural history--Juvenile literature. 7. Evolution (Biology)--Juvenile literature. I. Diemert, Katherine, illustrator II. Title.

QE501.25.G53 2017   j550   C2016-908276-8

Library of Congress Control Number: 2016962528

The artwork in this book was made using a mix of ink, collage, and digital media.

Edited by: Debbie Rogosin
Designed by: Karen Powers

Manufactured in Shenzhen, China, in March 2017, by C&C Joint Printing Co.

Job #HQ7398

A   B   C   D   E   F

Publisher of Chirp, chickaDEE and OWL | Owlkids Books is a division of Bayard
www.owlkidsbooks.com   CANADA